SLIDES IN A CAROUSEL

JEAN CARDY

CONTENTS

INTRODUCTION

This is the second book of a two-book collection of poems I have written over a period of about seventy years. I have had three books of poetry published and a few other books. I have had a varied and interesting career as teacher, lecturer and lecturer on a post-graduate course. I am a widow, with children and grandchildren so I have known family bereavement and joy. I have always lived in London but when my children were grown up, my husband and I travelled widely all over the world and I have relations in Canada, Australia and Tblisi .

I grew up under the shadow of WW1. In my childhood, the Spanish Civil war showed us how wars can arise and devastate countries. Then we had WW2 and the Blitz, evacuation and the constant expectation of invasion. After the war I was sent by the Foreign Office into war-devastated Germany as part of a team of three. There are echoes of some of these experiences in my poems.

Acknowledgements

My son-in-law, Paul Riches, suggested these books and has done an enormous amount in helping to compile and publish them.

Jean Cardy August 2021

1

DENIZENS

Mice live in the London Tube.
A train leaves
And small pieces of sooty black
Detach themselves from the sooty black walls
And forage for crumbs
In the rubbish under the rails
That are death to man.
You can't see their feet move.
They scurry like clockwork mice
And then they accelerate,
Faster than any clockwork mouse,
Faster than the eye can follow,
Your eye jerks to catch up with them.
There are usually three.
You can tell when a commuter has spotted one.
He becomes alert, alive -
It makes you realize the half-world
The other passengers exist in.
Once, a mouse came up on the platform

And sat, cleaning his whiskers,
Watched by a silent circle
Of respectful giants,
Tall as Nelson's Column.

LOUIS WAIN'S CATS

Louis Wain drew cats,
charming cats,
funny cats,
cats various,
cats hilarious,
cats winsome,
cats appealing,
sentimental cats,
realistic cats,
cats for the delectation,
cats for the admiration,
of the Edwardian public.

Louis Wain went mad
and, caged in an asylum,
covered wall after wall
with hundreds and hundreds
of close-packed cats.
The authorities had the sense
to leave them there.

But before madness chained him,
one night, after dinner at his club,
Wain drew, for the entertainment of members,
lightning sketches of cats.
Pressed to continue,
he covered a sheet
with furious scribble and scrawl.
Diners, a little embarrassed,
supposed him to be drunk,
or annoyed at being pestered.

Then, out of the random mess of lines,
gradually,
peered the head of a boy,
with a face so ancient in evil,
so alive with hatred and malice,
that the room fell silent.
Men left to go home
uneasily.

3

THE RE-ENACTORS

I have visited an Anglo-Saxon village
in a wood near Croydon,
watched a Civil War battle
where even the much-needed stretcher-bearers
rushed onto the field in costume.
Now Wellington's army has set up camp
in the Royal Festival Hall.
Greenjackets and Redcoats drill,
fire muskets out towards the high-rise flats.
Surgeons perform grisly battlefield operations.
Women endlessly wash clothes,
keep tents immaculate.
Addressed, they are knowledgeable,
always resolutely in character:
'Respectable married woman, ma'am,
Subject to the same discipline as the men.
If we misbehaves we gets flogged.'
It's a wonderful hobby.
It must take over your life.
Even your children join in.

But what does it do to your psyche,
I wonder, to spend so much time
wearing the clothes, eating the food,
speaking the dialect, practising the skills
of a bygone age?
Dp you return to our own with reluctance?
Or relief, if only because
we now have anaesthetics.

FOR GEORGE

The mynah in the hotel bar,
forever asking "What's your name?"
mimics each voice that taught him speech,
recording with a trick of tongue
each trick of personality.
The boss, who thinks himself alone,
hawking and belching, pours a drink –
George registers his privacy.
The mumbled orders "Scotch" and "ale",
the old girls' visit from the Home,
clustered around him, quavering, "George",
the old dog's whine, the intercom,
the vacuum-cleaner - all are George.

But ever between spates of speech
George, ever seeking for his mates,
whistles and waits,
whistles and waits.
Then go up closely to the cage,

a silent flustered bird withdraws.
That quizzing eye is all a fake,
a trick of feathers on the side,
caged in bird-mind, behind bird-eye,
George imitates our loneliness.

IN PRAISE OF PHATIC COMMUNION

"Phatic communion" sounds like some fancy religion
but it's the term for those little exchanges
that follow the first greetings –
"Nice day, isn't it?"
not meant as serious conversation,
not meant to be taken too far.
Someone who gives you a detailed account
of conflicting weather reports
is breaking the rules.
All countries do it, it seems
but different countries use different subjects.
In England, of course, it's the weather.
We have so much of it
and we're mocked for it.
In Sweden they talk of the weather too.
In Germany it's health –
just "I'm fine, thanks"
not a detailed analysis of your latest woe.
In China it's "Have you eaten?"
Maybe it all sounds silly

but it's essential oil;
it lubricates exchanges.
After a bare "Good morning", "Good evening"
we think, "Oh, have I upset her?"
Phatic communion is a touch, a handshake,
a smoothing of edges.

6

THE EVOLUTION OF THE WOLF

How could I so deplore
the babying of dogs?
seeing it as degrading
the dignity of their ancestor, the wolf
even as I rumpled, stroked,
teased and romped with
and loved a dog.
Now I recognise
this glorious evolution from wolf
into the loving companion of man,
which delights in and delights humans,
 the gentle comforter of sadness,
sniffer out of cancer,
which senses its owner's coming
from a mile or so away
and gives that ecstatic welcome at the door.

7

PAVLOVA'S COSTUMES IN THE MUSEUM OF LONDON

Pavlova wore these flounces.
These goose feathers
Fluttered in a swan's death,
One wing left loose
For the dancer's hand to simulate
That dying tremble.
The skirts grew shorter
As time passed,
Supported on American tarlatan,
With softer undulation
Than modern nylon.
Bakst designed this dress;
Madame Mayna created it
On this dressmaker's form.
Hips and waist were small
But bust nicely rounded -
No modern anorexic here.
Her feet were size 4 and narrow
All that leaping failed
To coarsen and broaden.

And she was Russian
So there is one costume,
Long, heavy with jewels,
Collared,
Topped with a crescent headdress,
Tarnished gold in a bow
At the back,
Almost too heavy to dance in,
Worn only at those private functions
Where she helped to raise funds
For the wounded Russian soldiers
She cared about.

We came to breathe a legend,
Stayed to admire
The underpinning of that legend -
Sequins, sewn, not glued,
Ballet shoes, herring-boned to control
The bulge of a foot en pointe,
Giselle's wings, sprayed
To evoke mystery,
Steel bands
To be hidden under hair
To support shimmering
Fairytale headdresses,
Giant hooks
To keep trim bodices taut.
Curators handle these things
In white gloves,
Not to harm,
Not to be harmed either -
Where have these costumes been
In their long history?

Nothing is ever cleaned -
Grubby muslin, crumpled flowers,
Missing jewels -
Pavlova wore these flounces.

THE COMFORT OF STATISTICS

Having lived through the Blitz
I am used to using statistics
for comfort.
If I feel at all nervous
when going up to London
after a terrorist attack
I remind myself
that in a city of millions
it is unlikely to be me.
"If it hasn't got your name on it"
as they used to say.
But I do sometimes think,
"Let it be me".
I am very old and expendable –
not my child or my grandchild
nor anyone dear to me.
No. Not any child.
Let it be me.

9

LAST TIME?

Will that be the last time?
The last time I swim in the sea?
In the warm Adriatic,
deep water to swim in,
just a yard or two off-shore,
then a barbecue on the beach:
sea-bass on bruschetti,
sausages, melon, and a rum baba
that was just
feather-light torn-off bits of bread
dipped in rum.
A fast boat-ride back –
wind and spray in one's face,
laughing with delight.

FASHION

Are you a slave of fashion?
No, of course not –
you dress to please yourself, don't you?
You know what suits you.
But Fashion herself
is not quite the elegant lady we imagine,
twirling in iridescent fabrics, lush colours;
She is a puppet;
the moguls pull her strings.
Once everyone has bought a mini-skirt,
Lo! ankle-length is what we must wear.
Aubergine baths are old hat –
it's back to clinical white.
That lovely lady has metamorphosed
into an octopus with slimy tentacles
slithering into everything.
Someone invents Sticky Toffee Pudding;
suddenly it's on every menu,
sold in every supermarket,
"because the customers demand it."

The most subservient slave of fashion
is that inveterate battler for freedom
the teenager;
crucial is the right stud
in the right part of the body,
the right slit in the jeans,
the right slang, the right swear words,
the right video games, the right trainers.
And above us all sit the moguls
dexterously manipulating the strings,
creating demands
to the music of money falling into tills.

A POET'S LAMENT

Actors, even busy ones,
at the end of each run, wonder,
"Will I ever work again?"
Poets are the same.
Poems come when they choose.
Few of us can write to order.
As you type out each poem, you think,
"Will that be the last?"
And poems are like buses;
after a long gap, three come together;
as happened today.

12

THE BEGINNER

The stage is full of empty chairs
with thin black legs
like a company of giant ants.
The audience gathers.
The woman in the floral dress,
who attends every concert,
takes her place
in the middle of the front row.
The musicians come on,
easy, relaxed, chatting, joking,
sublime music their everyday bread and butter.
Black and white formality makes a foil
for the glinting brass, gleaming wood
of their instruments:
aubergine double-bass,
cellos and violins in sherry,
chestnut, ripe apricot.

Then the conductor enters.
The orchestra rises in respect

but the boy knows
his baton must attempt to command
professors of music, soloists in their own right,
veterans, already experienced
when he learned his first scales.
He remembers the rituals: the bows,
the handshakes, how you must never
mop the trickling sweat.
He is wearing his first "tails",
wrinkling, restricting, shoulder-pads protruding,
making you realize the tailor's art
which will fashion those silken glissandos
he will present to the audience
when he can afford them.

He conducts fussily,
looks like a rugby player,
then, by the second movement,
Beethoven takes over.
Music dances through his body,
his hands, his baton.
He exchanges a grin of complicity
with his players.
He'll do.

13

AETIOLOGY

Today I learned a new word –
Aetiology means the projection of modern ideas
Into the past.
Your mind, which leapt to meet
Each new thing you encountered,
Is now stranded in the past,
Your feet are trapped in concrete.
As I am carried away from you,
Your figure achingly tiny in the distance,
I project every new concept
Back to the touchstone of your judgement.
But the world changes.
Soon, if I live, I shall encounter
Things outside the parameters
Of your experience;
I must trudge on alone.

LONDON MOON

The huge moon,
suspended low in the sky
in the gap between
the Royal Festival Hall
and the National Theatre,
illuminates a silken Persian
hanging carpet of golden mist.
Flat, like a Christmas chocolate penny,
round like a balloon,
alien like an Alien,
it dims the OXO sign,
the river lights,
the floodlit buildings,
then it bobs along the roofs
of the South Bank,
peeping over,
like a Smiley face,
beauty gone, but fun,
like a man so great

he can forget greatness,
laugh like a child,
clown with a child.

15

YULE SONG

Long ago, a child,
alone in the forest, lost,
I saw a glimmer of light,
struggled towards it,
found a clearing,
a great fire.
Hands welcomed me,
warmed me,
fed me.

Now, myself Lord of the Yule,
my hand cut the throat of the ox
on which we feast;
my hand set fire
to the great Yule log;
my voice welcomes friends and strangers,
blood-feuds set aside or ended;
my little son is Lord of Misrule,
licensed for a day to tease and trick
even his stately warrior brothers;

my wife sits enthroned,
Queen of the Feast,
in a little shelter of branches
bedecked with holly,
hands idle for a day,
accepting gifts,
suckling our newborn.

Once in a long while,
a traveller emerges from the trees,
stands, doubtful of welcome,
Is welcomed,
tells us tales of Yuletide
in far-off lands,
of a cold North country,
where the Lord of the Yule
is himself a traveller,
a shaman, wearing the red of shamans.
On the night of midwinter
he climbs the ice-houses,
lets down gifts through the smoke-hole,
accepts food and drink,
returns to his sledge.

From another land,
a hot country,
come tales of a baby king,
poorly born,
and a Queen of Midwinter,
receiving gifts from kings, star-led.

My seers, they of the mistletoe,
tell me of future men

who will fly like birds,
tunnel like moles,
swim below the seas,
send magic through the air -
but the seasons will still turn;
The People still need
to break the long dearth of Winter
with a celebration of the longest night
and the hope of Spring,
with a time of feasting and amity.

16

LIFE

In great whorls
Life swirls through the universe,
flashing blue fire.
You leap, when you can,
gain a footing,
balance,
exhilarated by the rush of air,
then jump, or fall, off
and watch for a time,
in the shadows,
thinking, with wonder,
"I used to do that,"
then fade.

EVENTS IN A CHILDREN'S WARD

The three-year-old toughie
charges his truck
up and down, up and down
the A & E children's ward.
Sometimes he pushes his way
into the glass-walled room
where his future is being broken up.
Sometimes his mad mother
slams out of the room,
screaming her fury
at not being allowed
to see her own child.
I pity her loss,
pity a child left
to her violent, raging love.
Once, she crashes through the heavy doors
into the outside world
and he follows her.
The watching mothers shout a warning
and the security guard hurries

to bring him back.
I wonder what the other small children
make of all this.
It's the eleven-year-old at my side
who notices the nasty scar
and mutters "Abuse."
I remark that people watch this sort of thing
on television, for entertainment, and she says,
"Well, it is...dramatic."
Finally the tired nurse and social worker leave
 and he starts to go off
with his exhausted aunt, father
and swollen-eyed grannie.
Suddenly he goes round the other truck-racers
and tries to say polite goodbyes
but they look at him blankly.
When he's a big burly chap
he'll make contact with us all
in more dangerous ways.

18

TODAY'S HEROES

Have you noticed
that all our greatest heroes today are black?
There are plenty of others, of course,
but those honoured worldwide:
Ghandi, Martin Luther King, Mandela, Obama
are all black. And all men,
though Aung   was among them until recently
but now there are questions, doubt
disappointments, sadness.
We revere the courage of our heroes
in the face of the constant threat of assassination,
their steadfastness, their dignity –
Remember Mandela emerging from prison,
Ghandi, who was once a figure of fun,
a butt for cartoonists.
They share a grace, a generosity of spirit –
Mandela enabling South Africa
to throw off apartheid
without the bloodbath we all feared
They had vision –

Obama for a juster America,
Ghandi for unarmed protest.
They had the gift of words
to convince people of that vision;
remember Martin Luther King
at Newcastle University, making, off-the-cuff, impromptu
an oration so powerful it encompassed
all those ideals of ending racism, poverty and war
which they shared.
And this was no list of banal platitudes;
it was empowered with phrases like,
'The law cannot make a man love me
but it can restrain him from lynching me.'
and the desire to
'Transform the jangling discord of our nation.'

CATHERINE WHEEL

Family row,
the one and only
fail-safe Catherine Wheel,
ignites at a match
fizzes, twirls spins,
a fiery circle
spitting off
flesh-shreds, memories
fragmented peace,
most satisfying,
while it lasts.

Leaving
a garden unillumined,
skewed wire,
sour smoke.

CROCUSES ON THE ESTATE

"Don't buy a house down there," they said,
"It's near The Estate,"
and the two words contained,
like an anagram,
shadowy hooded menace
and feckless Daily Mail nightmare.

Now, in sunny February,
I track a way over the estate
(deliberately complex, to prevent through traffic)
to reach the fields and brook beyond.
There's a river walk you can follow for miles
and a tree with parakeets.
It's country, so you greet people and smile.
Little houses on the estate open on to this;
blocks of flats look over it.
One tiny garden has a tall palm tree.
The brook eventually makes it
to the Thames.
True, someone has dumped two kids' bikes

in the water.

True, the generous stretches of inviting grassland
tend to say, "No Ball Games"
but then someone, the Council?,
has planted all over them
in unregimented profusion
yellow and purple crocuses
that lift the heart.

21

SASKIA

"Wriggle bottom."
"I *not*. I Saskia."
"Noisy oyster."
"I *not*. I Saskia.
"Sweetheart
Honey pot.
Pigsneye."
"I *not*.
I *not*.
I *not*
I *Saskia*."

Good to have such a cast-iron
Copper-bottomed
Rock-hard
Sense of your own identity.

But Daddy calls her Sasky.

THE DANCE OF MEMORY

When you are as old as I am,
Memory leads you a wobbly dance.
Museum-pieces are objects
familiar from childhood –
mangles, dishes for jam and butter,
Liberty bodices.
Events like wars
that are history to others
Are childhood memories
The Depression is an uncle always out of work,
your mother answering the phone
to another desperate plea for money.
The Spanish Civil War meant
collecting for milk for Spanish babies,
a school debate,
understanding that this was a different war
where the established government, under attack,
was Left, of the people,
not, as usual, the other way round
grasping that the bombs were probably our future,

being deeply impressed
when our Classics mistress
brought back a husband,
Colonel in the Republican army,
glamorous in tricorne hat
and swirling black cloak.
And WW2 was our war:
evacuation, the sound of bombs whistling down,
initial fear of gas,
fear of imminent invasion,
shrapnel banging on the shelter door
snores drowning sleep in an indoor Morrison shelter.
All these are vivid as yesterday
but to follow-up questions
Memory often refuses any answers
but then, singing nursery rhymes to a baby great grandson
seeing him suckle,
suddenly there are vivid physical memories
of the joy of feeding your own,

THE SADNESS OF LULLABIES

Lullabies are love-songs,
mother to child,
"Go to sleep, my darling,
safe in my arms."
So why are the melodies of lullabies so sad?
Perhaps every mother,
like Mary before her,
gazes on her sleeping child,
fearing its fate,
crooning and keening,
"Hush-a-bye, my darling,
rocked in my arms,
never so secure again
'gainst a cruel world."

24

EMPIRE

If graceful withdrawal
is the prime virtue in retirement
then perhaps one is permitted
a last lingering pride in empire -
that we have been able to relinquish it
so quickly, almost so completely.
I remember lessons as a child
where the red bits were pointed out
on a huge wall-map
and one heard, "The sun never sets."
There was Empire Day,
when we marched around the playground
waving flags,
the biggest flags going first,
mingy ones at the back.
Now, save for apologies,
who remembers Empire?
There was the period of surprise
when citizens of empire
took us at our word

and came to "The Motherland"
expecting welcome.
There was the time,
before we understood our new status,
the time of Suez,
when "Send a gun-boat"
was still the panacea,
then a time when "Empire"
morphed into "Commonwealth";
now Commonwealth is the domain
of faded royals making tours
past children asking,
"Who is that lady in a hat?"
One would rejoice
but that the inheritors of Empire
are vast global businesses,
still ignoring local laws, local rights,
the just payment of taxes,
the welfare of peoples.

THE DUTIES OF MOTHERHOOD

"Mum, I've got to be a zebra
for assembly tomorrow."
"Will mothers kindly collect the carrier-bags
marked with their child's name
and sew their costumes
for the Nativity play."
"Mum, Miss MacMullen says,
will you make these cardboard boxes
into a cave for the Wicked Witch."

At those antenatal classes
where they teach you
all about breathing and stuff
why doesn't someone say,
"And you've got to be able
to sew and stick,
paste and paint?

When they talk of the underprivileged
they forget about kids

with a mum like me,
whose cardboard castles always collapse,
whose plaster bulb-bowls always leak,
whose lopsided costumes never fit,
who made Mother Mary
look like a miniscule bag-lady.

And now, of course, you've got to be
a computer whizzkid as well.

THE COPPER CANDLESTICKS

Two copper candlesticks
stand on my mantel piece,
one of them slightly bent.
In the first world war
my father led a troop
into a village just won from the Germans.
Two old women
were offering the candlesticks for sale.
They told my father
they were ancient family heirlooms.
buried to save them from the "sale boche"
He said he could not deprive them of family heirlooms
but they said, "We must sell them.
We need to eat."
So he gave them twice what they asked
and now they gleam on my mantel piece
with a history,
Goodness knows how old.

MALE DISPLAY

In the animal kingdom,
almost without exception,
males display
to attract the favours
of drab females..
They dance, dapper in bright colours –
baboons' faces and rumps,
fish stripes.
Only amongst humans
Is this reversed –
females are mostly
more colourful than males
and live in fear of
attacks or rape by males.
So how or why or when
did all this change
so that now it is dangerous
for a woman to walk alone at night?

28

CAUTIOUS OPTIMISM

In spite of racial football chants,
attacks on gays,
swastikas daubed on synagogues,
despite all this,
things really have moved on:
counting-out games don't
"catch a nigger by his toe";
homophobes begin to understand
it's their own urges they fear;
princes don't shoot tigers;
wearing fur provokes
contempt, not envy;
no-one would speculate today
whether mixed-race Colin Powell might have
"a touch of the tar-brush";
bullying in school or home
is at least recognised, not ignored;
no baby's labelled "bastard."

Not long ago,

all these were commonplace, unquestioned;
few saw anything wrong,
so what do we do or say today,
I wonder,
that we shall blush for tomorrow?

TWELFTH NIGHT

So, it's over, Christmas.
Tinsel and lights stashed away
ready for next year.
Dead names crossed off
from the Christmas card list.
Time to look out
over the bleak landscape.
Time to reflect
that our "midwinter celebration"
comes when Winter has scarcely begun.
Two months of snow and flu
and icy roads
still to trudge through
and that's for those of us
in warm houses, safe jobs.
How will they make out,
those others,
those bundles of clothes and blankets
huddled in corners of city streets –

rich cities, rich streets
now celebrating their next ritual –
the January sales?

"I'M NOT A FEMINIST BUT…"

Yes, well, all right,
so life is not perfect,
so there are still mistakes,
heart-breaks, bad decisions,
but have you ever thought,
can you imagine
what it was like
to have a brain
trapped in a woman's body
in, say, 1850?
Yes, if you were a Nightingale
you could retire to your bed,
get things done,
exercise power
but for most
it was little education
or none,
twelve kids, often an early death.
Worse still
if you "strayed",

had a "love-child"
or just provoked talk,
the shame, the descent.
So be thankful;
things are better,
much better,
but not everywhere.
Let's talk Saudi,
talk Taliban,
worse there for some women
than anywhere in our own past history,
so why is it fashionable
to sneer at feminism?
"I'm not a feminist but.."
Well, you ought to be –
there are battles still to fight.

31

AGING

Sudden the beach shelves –
I ride the scree-fall.
Shingle helter-skelters –
I keep my footing.
Tide drags feet from under.
Fingers scrabble jobs, promotion,
offspring, status, skill.
Mind welters; back flays.
In breakers of sand, boulders,
aphasia, arthritis, hiatus hernia.
Sea is kind, swells, bubbles.
The ocean is empty.

TREADING A BATTLEFIELD

There's a place in Essex,
Maldon, on the estuary,
where the yachtsmen go.
You can tread the paths
described by a poet
more than a thousand years ago.
 A battle was fought there
in the year nine hundred and ninety one.
Norsemen sailed up the Blackwater,
landed on Northey Island
and waited for the tide to go out
so they could cross the causeway –
it's still there –
and reach the mainland
and give battle to the Anglo-Saxons
awaiting them there
in the field you cross.
Both sides shouted challenges, threats, insults.
My husband and I stood,
one on Northey

and one on the mainland
and hurled insults at each other,
laughing, just to show it could be done,
though mostly we felt respect
for what had gone on there.
A young English warrior was reprimanded
for bringing his hawk to battle,
not taking his role seriously,
so he unleashed his hawk,
let it fly free to the wood
that still grows there
at the end of the battlefield –
a great sacrifice
since to man a hawk
you had to walk three days and nights,
 unsleeping, the hawk on your wrist,
feeding it bits of meat
so it grew accustomed
to being attached to you.
The Norsemen trounced the English
who gathered round their leader,
Byrhtnoth. As they died, one by one,
someone called out:
"As our number lytleth (grows smaller)
so must our hearts and courage be the greater."

33

INTIMATIONS OF MORTALITY

How should a child be acquainted with death?
The secure, the middle-class way,
conducts solemn obsequies
for guinea pig or sparrow –
two crossed sticks
stuck in the grave.
Tomorrow we buy a new pet.
In a religious home, the child is comforted
with tales of angels, heavenly reunions
(though with some doubts
concerning the admission of dogs.)
But what of the child who loses
parent, playmate, sibling, twin –
acquainted with death too young?
Do you offer comfort
with lies you don't believe?
And what of the child caught up in horror –
tsunami, earthquake, fire, war?
How can the child
who has seen his world swept away,

trust again
when death waits at every crossroad,
on every stony beach,
wherever the dark-cloaked stranger
turns his gaze
of bleak selection?

34

CONVERSATION ON A RAILWAY STATION IN SRI LANKE – A TRUE STORY

"Mummy, why is that man looking at me?"
"Well, darling, you've got fair hair –

They're not used to fair hair here."
"People keep touching my hair. I don't like it."
"Pretty child. Pretty child. I buy."
"You must be joking."

"I not joking. Pretty child. I buy.
I give you twenty pound."

"Christ, Pete, he's not joking.
Hold on to her."

"You want more? I give you more.
I give you thirty, forty pound."

"Daddy, Daddy, don't hold me so tight.
You're hurting me!"

"You sure? You sure you not sell?
I give you fifty pound."

"Daddy, why is Mummy crying?
Why is that little girl screaming?
Why is she going off with that nasty man?
Is he her Daddy?"

"No, darling, he's not her Daddy.
That's her Daddy over there,
That man walking away."

"Did the nasty man take her instead of me?
Because she's got black hair?"

Well, in a way, yes, darling."
"Is she five, like me?"
"Yes, I should think so, yes."

35

CULTURAL ADVENTURE IN THE CAUCUSUS

As a child tiptoes,
in fairy story or dream,
through corridors, round corners
in a palace? a wizard's lair?,
not knowing what she will find –
a dragon? a king?
so I endeavour to enter
your culture, so different from mine,
soon to be so important to me.

I am moved with compassion
for a country so fought over,
so torn between competing powers
as vultures will tear a prey apart,
a country bridging Asia and Europe.
I learn a little of the language
but cannot read
the graceful, impenetrable script.
I consult books
but ask myself

Is this still true?
Is it true only in the mountains?

My work used to move me
to different towns
and I used to remind myself
"In a few days, weeks,
this will all be familiar;"
so I tell myself now
but there is a difference –
a culture is so vast, so subtle
a lifetime is too short
to learn it deeply –
and that's where the excitement lies.

DEMONS

Heaney and the Beowulf poet
Told in the London Tube
Of a powerful demon, a prowler in the dark,
Nursing a hard grievance.
In the seat below,
A tall handsome macho black man
Clutched his comfort blanket
Mumbled enquiries about where he was,
Where we were going,
Lurched to his feet at Warren Street station.
As he queued to get off,
He began to cry, wail, sob,
Stood on the platform
Head raised like a wolf,
Howling his world sorrow.
Concern shifted through the carriage
Like an uneasy wind.
The train moved on.
There was nothing we could do.
Nothing. Nothing.

"TEA OR COFFEE?"

Coffee tastes horrible,
if your mouth expects tea
and vice versa.
So it is with our loves and likings;
expecting the smooth and bland,
we are affronted
by blunt outspokenness.
South calls North crude;
North thinks South
stuck-up, two-faced.
But even the expected
may be rejected
as boring, always the same.
And sometimes we crave the outré,
the bizarre, the paradoxical.
Foodwise, humans, like foxes
flourish as omnivores.
Can we evolve a little further,
and extend this to people?
embrace diversity?

WHAT SHALL WE DO
WITH HABEUS CORPUS?

What shall we do with Habeus Corpus?
Trial by judge or trial by jury?
What shall we do with any trial at all?
Drown them in Guatanamo Bay.

What shall we do with the concept of innocence?
Access to charges, evidence or lawyers?
Confessions inadmissible obtained under duress?
Dump them in Guantanamo Bay.

What shall we do with the rule of law?
What shall we do with civilisation?
What shall we do with freedom and justice?
Chuck them in Guantanamo Bay.

FRONTIERS

Countries are nervous at the edges.
They dread not only bomb and gun,
Drugs, alien plants, rabid dogs, terrorists,
But also alien ideas, subversive texts, candy.
At a refuelling stop in Minneapolis,
Huge uniformed women
Stood in the shopping mall
Thundering that it was forbidden
To introduce **any** foodstuffs
Into the USA.
Soviet officials, still almost boys,
Were trained to stare, unsmiling,
Back and forth,
Between you and your passport,
Reducing the most innocent
To shifty guilt.

Then you have to remember
Which countries you **have** been to
Which might offend the susceptibilities

Of the country you **want** to enter,
So you proffer little bits of paper
To be stamped
And scan your passport
For incomprehensible stamps
In alien alphabets
That might give you away.

I stayed with friends in Jerusalem,
Having recently visited Jordan.
That did it.
On the way out of Israel
The quiet young girl in uniform
Questioned me endlessly.
Where had I stayed?
Who else did I know?
Whom had I met?
How had I got to know them?
How had I got to know
The friends in England
Who introduced us?
"It was thirty years ago," I protested.
At last I realized that normal conversational good manners -
Editing your replies of unnecessary detail -
Were not appropriate here.
So in the manner of my ancient aunts
I settled down to answer her questions
With every tedious detail and correction
I could think of
Until finally I bored her
Into letting me go.

Countries recently opened up to tourists

Are the most nervous;
To get into Libya
You have to fill in a form
To apply for permission
To fill in a form
To apply for a visa.
Coming out, we had been warned of strip-searches -
By male staff on female tourists.
When we were pulled out of the hours-long queue
We feared the worst
But our clever, worldly-wise, Libyan guide
Was clearly making use
Of the dotty eccentric amongst us
Who had been his bane -
"You don't want to tangle with **her**!"
Much laughter and back-slapping and we were through.

Sometimes you get caught up
In private hostilities between neighbouring countries;
Crossing Czechoslovakia
In Soviet times
We were woken twice at each border
In the early hours,
Ordered to open cases
In cramped bunks
While a guard twirled a gun
Round one finger
As in a Western.

Albania to Yugoslavia was the worst.
Going into Albania - no religious objects,
No beards, no pornography -
Such as a Times photograph

Of a nude Adam
In the Sistine chapel.
Coming out of Albania, at dawn,
A New Zealand girl knew she had to have
The exact money for a visa -
She had.
It must be in Yugoslavian currency -
It was.
Ah! triumph! one note was not pristine
And therefore unacceptable.

But as somebody said,
It's no good going abroad
To see a different world
And then complaining
Because things are not
Just like home.

40

COACH PARTIES

Our hair is grey, or white.
We wear sensible shoes.
Some of us walk with sticks.
We are the coach parties.
Organised by the National Trust,
The University of the Third Age
numerous art and history societies,
we visit castles, stately homes.
There are not many men amongst us.
Looking round, they must wonder
how long they will survive
into this world of widows.
It pleases me
that I can pay my entrance fee
and invade these domains
of ancient titles,
vast wealth, parks
and pleasure gardens,
family portraits –
all strictly closed, in the past

to the likes of me.

We have our aches and pains,
our twinges,
but we are a lucky generation.
Our artificial hips and knees,
our hearing aids,
our pensions
allow us a golden age,
mostly denied even to the rich
who owned these grand houses.
Denied, sadly, perhaps,
to our successors.
We live too long.
There are too many of us
The young begin to resent us.

41

UNKNOWN GENTLEMAN

Elegant in black velvet,
Long fingers resting on sword hilt,
Background of park and hounds,
This lord of lands
Stares with disdain
At the dauber
He has commissioned
To ensure his futurity.
The companion piece, of his wife,
Is not quite satisfactory;
Haughty to all but her lord,
Still there is a hint
Of something else -
Amusement? Complicity?
Now they hang together in the gallery -
Portrait of a Gentleman Unknown,
Portrait of a Lady ditto.
And the dauber?
Ah, see the name in gold -

Velasquez,
Titian,
Van Dyck -
He sat for them all,
That unknown gentleman.

42

NORFOLK

I see Norfolk with a stranger's eyes,
belonging, as I do, to mountains or cities.
A flat land this, of marshes and sea-birds,
a place of great men's houses,
Holkham, Houghton, Sandringham,
which eat up the land
or maybe conserve it?
Deferential cottages cluster at their gates.
A land of vast skies for painters
and vast shores for birders,
surveying the astonishing Wash,
where the sea recedes out of sight,
leaving mudflats dotted
with scavenging shelducks,
like white beads
scattered from a broken string.
But Norfolk is a friendly place
and now I remember
a great-grandmother from Wisbech,

a husband's forebears from Suffolk,
connections not far to seek
as for most of us in this small island.
We are a mongrel race
and the better for it.

43

STILL ALIVE

Visiting my father in his final days,
I would ask conventionally, "How are you?"
The answer in those last, bed-ridden days,
was always "Still alive".
Then in my busy prime
I was too young, too green, too naïve
to recognise
the invitation, the plea, the need
to talk about his death,
about the great unknown he was facing.

And still today, when we pride our selves
 that we can talk without inhibition,
about all the forbidden subjects –
periods, the menopause, sexual abuse
yet death is still verboten –
"Don't be morbid".
Even practical things like trying to send to Oxfam
some of the hoard of possessions

accumulated and forgotten over many years,
to ease the task of clearing up after my death,
even that is greeted with
"You don't want to think about things like that yet."
(No, wait until you're too far gone to do it!)

44

THE SEVEN AGES OF WOMAN

First the pink stage –
party dresses and dolls.
Or tomboy.
Or both.
Then teenage moods,
make-up, boys, war with mum.
Later, nascent learning,
ambition, radical thoughts.
Then embarkation on a career and a love-life.
Followed by marriage, kids,
the chat at the school gate.
Then the exciting, demanding,
breathless, exuberant bit –
combining work you love,
family you love.
That's if you're lucky, very lucky
and don't live in Saudi Arabia
or poverty.
As children grow, it calms a little;
now you are confident in what you do.

Next retirement and U3A and rich opportunity,
delight in new role as grandmother,
some impediments, deafness mainly,
some health problems,
too busy to worry overmuch,
friends die away.
Finally, who knows? –
Dementia? Stuck in a home,
watching daytime telly?
Well, that's nine stages
but we live longer than men
so why not?
And that's if we have been lucky, so lucky.

45

ASTRONOMERS ARE POETS

Astronomers are poets;
by metaphor, simile, analogy,
they strive to awaken the earth-bound
to distances, numbers, stretches of time
beyond our imaginations.

So Carl Sagan tells us there are more stars
in the universe than grains of sand
on all the beaches on earth.
For two and a half thousand years at least
astronomers have striven
so to enlighten us,
battling, often, with the blindness
of myth, of religion
and of Man's clinging to his own importance,

Man as the centre of a world
that is the centre of the universe.
And astronomers are poets too
in their language, fired by

their excitement and delight;
Sagan talks of the death of stars
flashing on and winking off
like fireflies in the night.

Man has always looked at the stars,
wondered about them, told stories;
now giant telescopes show us
rings and moons and colours
we could never see before
and astronomers try to share with us
their vision.

WASTED LIVES

There's an abandoned bungalow in my road;
brambles reach over the pavement;
retaining walls threaten collapse.
I fume at the waste of a potential home.
Only it isn't abandoned.
Two brothers live there. Recluses.
Their lives impossible to imagine
as those of whales, moles, Amazonian Indians,
or the quiet little commuter
who makes the same journey,
does the same job,
goes home to the same house,
from leaving school to retirement.
Then you read the obituaries;
there are lives where trumpets sound,
banners unfurl,
colours splash on canvas,
wild roads are travelled.
Sad that some lives are tossed away
like crumpled bus tickets.

THE SUCCESSES OF GIRLS

Girls consistently out-perform boys.
So spare a lament for all those women
throughout aeons of history
and still in many cultures
who are denied the rich education of boys,
assumed always to be second-rate,
interested only in trivia.
Often they had babies so young
and so often
there was no room in their lives
for anything else.
A few, like Florence Nightingale, Madame Curie,
by sacrifice, wiles or luck,
managed to make their mark.
Some, like Byron's daughter,
showed their scientific inventiveness,
before an early death.
Some, like her, and the first Elizabeth
received an education.
But for most, how their brains

must have boiled in turmoil
within their heads
with the desire
to question, understand,
give voice to ideas,
while the men brought the world
to the danger of extinction.

48

TEARS ARE A GIFT OF LOVE

Tears are a gift of love.
We shared a journey
from nowhere to nowhere,
deep in soft cushions,
drowsy with sun,
lulled by the distant jazz of the wheels,
private from all the world,
on our journey from nowhere to nowhere.
You gave me a story
of earnest youth,
tramping the roads
to try a vocation,
standing outside a post office,
lacking, for stiff conscience,
the price of a stamp.

Tears surprised me.
Ridiculous, for such a deprivation.
Being young, I was discomfited
until I saw your eyes

accepting the gift.
Those tears and a book
were all I could give you.
When the train clanked into somewhere
I walked away alone,
away through the barren bleak streets.

49

HEALING

I send you these notes
relayed mind to mind
my finger-tips pulsating with power -
a gift for your healing.

Crow rises clumsily, cumbrously,
made nervous by slow take-off;
wings struggle to lift heavy body.
Orchestra labours to crescendo
and I to lift you from the depths,
fingers pulsating but hard-tasked.
Then orchestra finds freedom;
strings, flutes, percussion
interlock in joy.
Gull soars, riding the air-waves,
barely a wing-flap,
gravity discarded.
My hands enclose your being,
relay mind to mind,

beg, command your spirit
to fly free and joyous –
a hope for your healing?

50

THE SCAM

Oh what a fool I am!
How could I fall for a scam?
I've fended off lots in the past.
I suppose that was not going to last.
Looking back, I have to admit
to admiring the skill just a bit
of the scammer who had me in thrall
in the course of a two-hour call
till I did just what I was told,
all my secrets began to unfold.
With his voice so honeyed and friendly
it was only when at the end he
insisted I must not tell
a soul that I heard the bell
warning me of the fleece
and rang the fraud police
so my cards were all stopped in time -
for the scammer no fruits for his crime.
The police said I wasn't to blame

though so near to disaster I came;
they said scammers are now so clever
not many escape them for ever
so forgive this use of verse
to warn of attacks on your purse!

51

BACK TO WORK

Outside Ilford station
when I was a child
the street was cobbled,
slippery.

The huge dray-horses
from the coal-yard
thrust their strong necks against heavy yokes,
scrabbled their giant feathered hooves,
struggling to get a purchase,
striking sparks – iron shoes against stone.

It seemed the loads of bulging, tarry sacks
would never move.
At last, under the lash,
wheels began to turn,
just a little, then more.
Soon the wagon was running sweetly,
not much effort needed now.

I used to recall that scene
at the start of every term.

52

MADNESS

"Harvested madness" –
the name Russell Brand gave
to Robin Williams' wild
"geyser " of comedy.
Maybe there's more
for all of us to harvest.
Maybe we should listen more
to the wild, the manic, the eccentric –
listen as well as seek to cure.
Maybe we should encourage
some self-harvesting.
But would there be things in the crop
to poison, not feed us?

53

FEAR

In the civilised world
most of us have lost the habit of fear.
We drive on roads
without thinking of the accident rate,
fly in planes, not fearing
they might fall out of the sky.
But there are times when fear is appropriate,
a warning it is time to take action,
to change our ways.
The climate crisis is destroying the planet
but we are not afraid enough
to give up our cars and planes.
Sometimes we learn the wrong lesson
from the past.
In 1939 you never went from one room to another
without your gas mask
because gas was the great dread
in the trenches of the previous war.
A temporary lull in our fears

when nothing much happened in that first year
and we relaxed our precautions
just in time for the next onslaught
as evacuated children came home -
all ready for the Blitz.

54

___

KIDDING

"My other car's a Porsche."

"Sorry, driver,
'Fraid I don't know the drill,
Don't know the stop -
See I usually take a cab."

"`Course I only do this to oblige.
When my dear husband was alive
I wouldn't have dreamed of taking paying guests
And now it's just a few
And very select.
Please wipe your feet.
No baths at night.
Children to be quiet at all times."

"Of course they just begged me to stay.
`We can't do without you,` they said,
But I said, `No, I've made up my mind,
I have to consider my health`

And the package they offered
I really couldn't refuse
But they begged me to stay,
`How shall we manage without you
To keep us in order?`
They said."

"I don't know why I'm overweight.
I really don't eat a thing.
It's my glands/metabolism/family history
Or perhaps it's my nice nature.
Does anyone want the last piece of cake?"

55

SWARMS

At Gatwick, you look down from your coffee
on the human swarm below:
people like bees, starlings, herring,
ants, wildebeest.
No, not a swarm.
Swarms are smooth, economical,
organised, all of one mind,
elegant.
Only humans crowd like this,
an ants' nest disturbed,
crisscrossing in all directions,
at different paces,
anxious, cluttered.
Too many choices.
It's not good to live like this.
I long for quiet and fresh air,
a green meadow.

56

WHAT DO YOU MEAN, I'M MEAN?

I wake in the dark
in the wake of a boozy wake
for the departed soul
of a colleague.
I was the sole woman there
and we ate battered sole,
followed by a light dessert
which didn't please the men
but they made light of it
and adjourned to a pub
to read some light verse
our friend had written.
He wasn't too bright, our friend,
so we were glad of the bright light
in the pub garden
to decipher his words.
In his will he left me a ring
which will fit on my little finger
but my husband will have a fit

and he might do all in his might
to make me get rid of it.
I think it is time to stop
so this is my final full stop.

57

XENOPHOBIA

Like a child defacing her picture-book
someone has splashed sour and strident yellow
across the English landscape.
By a happy homonym
"rape" they call it, Rape indeed.
The harmony of Constable colours,
subtle and varied greens and browns,
silvery or peaty streams,
all shifting and changing
with passing cloud patterns,
darkness of tree
and sheep-shadow –
all this is set jangling
by alien and discordant yellow,
jarring the landscape
making us all,
in this one respect,
xenophobic.

58

WAVES OF TRAGEDY

Tragedies spread across the ocean
in great waves
that end in ripples of discontent
on seaside beaches.
My cleaner irritated me
by loud continuous conversation
on her phone as she worked.
Then she brought a picture on her phone
of her Brazilian mother
to introduce us.
Later she told me that her parents
had gone camping three days before,
together with her mother's best friend
from when they were five years old.
The friend had slipped
into the fast-flowing river
and been carried away,
her body found two days later.
Graecia's mother was devastated
and her father, that he had not been

strong enough to save her friend.
Graecia had kept her mother on her phone,
following her around as she worked
to give her some companionship in her grief.
I was glad I had not voiced
my momentary irritation.

59

WHY WAR?

I grew up under the shadow
of the Great War. Father, five uncles
fought and survived. Just.
Every year, on the eleventh hour,
 of the eleventh day, of the eleventh month,
the world stopped. In schools, in the street,
we stood in silence, remembering the dead.
Teachers, aunts, wept a little
for lost husbands, lovers, brothers
but it was the war to end all wars
so it was worth it, wasn't it?
Then began the signs of another war to come.
My father, veteran of one war
joined the Home Guard,
picked up his tin hat and his rifle,
went off through the Blitz and the shrapnel
to mount dangerous guard
over a munitions factory.
I do not find Dad's Army funny.
Now, in a global world,

we commemorate the first of the world wars
but today there are wars everywhere –
Afghanistan, Syria, Israel, Ukraine
and to what end? And will it ever stop?
When will we find that elusive Peace?

60

ESTRANGED KITCHEN

"The best thing about cooking
in a stranger's kitchen
is going back to your own."
That should be framed and hung in my kitchen
where the bread bin is in the office,
underneath the wok
and the defunct dishwasher
is a very efficient filing cabinet.
After it died and I decided
someone living alone
really didn't need a dishwasher
I joked that I might find
very dirty dishes people had put
disintegrating inside.
And did.
So it now has a sign-
"Not in use" though it is in use
as a filing cabinet.
Lower shelves are over-crowded
and top shelves empty,

because I can't reach them now
and I wash up with rags
which are washed daily
and much more hygienic
but shock visitors.
Trouble is, when the kind strangers leave
I can't find anything either
because they are all in different places,
rational but wrong
or out of reach.

61

AN ATHEIST LOOKS BACK

It's tough when your faith relinquishes you –
a long painful process,
shouldering your way up
from a sucking, restraining quicksand,
to emerge on a cold, bleak beach,
bereft of a warm, sustaining hand.

For a time, even music
seems emptied of feeling
and no heavenly reunions await.
So now, looking back, after so many years,
what streaks are left from those days
of passionate belief?

And are they ugly, like bad make-up
or are some still radiant?
There is a certain amazement
that one can have held such beliefs –
did I really preach on street corners?

There's regret at opportunities missed,
because of a rigid morality,
for romance and experimentation.
What a frigid frump I must have been!

But in many ways a good morality too;
I thought it was Christian,
that belief that every human being is my sister or brother
and I owe them care
and indeed Christians may have done more than most
to spread that tenet widely,
though hardly universally, in the world.

The most enduring legacy of firm belief
is the habit of self-examination.
I query everything I do –
am I really being kind
or do I just want to appear so?

If the unexamined life is no life
the over-examined is irritating
and time-wasting.

Finally I have learned to accept that I am human.
Everything I do will have mixed motives.
What matters is to do what one can –
little bits of help, kindness.
Just get on with it.

62

STORM

During the war
my college was the guest of Balliol.
St Hugh's became a hospital
for head wounds
so Balliol lent us Holywell Manor.
Years later they invited us to a celebratory lunch
in the Manor garden.
What could be nicer? –
lunch in June in an Oxford garden.
The marquee shone with satin
like a sheik's palace.
Delicious food greeted us,
colourful as a painting –
great salmon decked out with tiny delicacies.
Then the storm struck.
Rain thundered on delicate satin.
Gales drove torrents
through the entrances.
Except for the lightning

it was too dark to see fish-bones.
Thunder drowned the speakers.
Whatever had we done
so to anger the gods?

63

AUTOROUTE

The names trudge past -
Blue signs on an autoroute -
Bapaume, Bethune, Arras.
We cross the tranquil Somme.
Fields lie flat between
The little towns.

Huge ploughs have turned the mud
Into rank upon rank of giant clods.
Earth colours change by district -
Dirty mustard, khaki, metallic grey.
The land is water-logged.
Small lakes form
As if you could still drown in it.
Summer tourists do not see this
As they speed past
Green fertile fields.

The coach falls silent.

Then someone says,
"There`s the turn-off for Dunkirk.
My brother came through there."

64

BLACK HOLES

They've found another black hole in the Milky Way
the size of one hundred thousand suns.
Or was it a hundred million?
It's not the biggest.
That's the size of four hundred thousand suns.
Or four hundred million.
They think one day
these black holes might amalgamate.
The imagination tries to encompass all this,
approaches, falters, shrivels away.
The pain in my neck
seems less important.
Even the threatened death
of our beautiful planet;
annihilated by climate change
or nuclear war
becomes a brief incident
in the billions of years
of the universe –
a slug confronted by a skyscraper.

But no, Not so.
Our gut feeling rebels.
Gaia is a good, a thing of beauty,
a jewel,
something we must nurture
must fight for
as long as we can

65

FACES IN THE FOYER

Faces, faces come at me: a war-dance of faces
rhythmically advance and retreat, the advance
the more inexorable. faces on the stage
not more inhumanly grotesque,
hostile, grey and white, remote, belligerent,
alien masks, than faces in the foyer.
faces, masks, come, go, advance,
retreat, in a war-dance, a dance of display,
a dance of some ugly, alien, predatory bird -
vulture, orc, roc; the display not perceptibly
sexual, but intellectual, posturing, pirouetting
bowing, stretching tall, to impress some equally alien,
equally cold, hostile, remote, unintelligible, pseudo-intel-
ligence.

I met the advancing, eyeless faces
because I quested yours. When you arrived,
a little anxious, a little hurried,
equally questing, there was peace, warmth,
friendship, memory of shared talk and children.

And is that all?
It is something.

It is a beaten-earth cave-floor
on which to crouch, in times of rough weather,
when humanity perforce preys on itself.
You don't fall below the floor.
Unless, of course, the earth cracks beneath you.
Short of that, you don't fall below the cave-floor.
And when the watery sun shines outside
you can come out, feel warmth, rejoice,
accepting the vagaries of the light
and this is better, much better,
than the warrior masks in the foyer.

But for some, one morning,
the familiar other figure
rises from the cave-floor
and raises the cold mask
and holds it in front of his face
even within the cave.

66

BRICK PAVEMENTS

In Tunbridge Wells
The streets are paved with brick,
Warm, neat, patterned,
Different from other pavements.
My mother told me so.

And I can see them now,
The bricks large and clearly defined
From my viewpoint of two feet tall.

Now two-year-old
Granddaughter
Inhabits that world of giants,
That world of knees and shins,
That world close to earth.
The garden is full
Of the excitement of Spring.
To her it is a world
Of tiny moving insects.

She calls me to see
Ants, ladybirds,
Spiders too small to fear,
So that even I can admire
Their black and white prettiness.

67

SILENCE IS PRECIOUS

Silence is precious –
the silence of a blazing summer Sunday afternoon;
a mountain lake high in Alaska;
a remote Shetland island.

What is better than silence?
Music, beloved voices,
falling water, birdsong,
a welcome key in the lock.

What is more exciting than silence?
Music for dance, a crowd rejoicing, thunder,
drums, cry of curlew, bittern, buzzard,
expectant buzz of a summer city street.

What is bad silence?
Unspoken, menacing anger,
tension in a failing aircraft,
the moment after impact
before the screaming starts.

What shatters silence?
The scream of a bomb descending,
screams of agony,
screams of a raging row.

When is silence most welcome?
Peace after quarrels,
escape from city cacophony,
the return home.

68

ECLIPSE ECLIPSED

It was to be our last chance
to see an eclipse
in our lifetime.
Warnings everywhere
not to damage eye-sight
by looking directly at the sun.
Friends flew off to the Faroes.
In the event
you couldn't even see
where the sun was in the sky.
The day began overcast
became more overcast
at the appointed time,
then less so.
And that was it.
Later, a blue tit disported itself,
twittering, in my camellias,
one red bush, one pink, entwined –
a delight to watch.
We learn in childhood

that the treat much anticipated
often inexplicably disappoints.
Perhaps only later we discover
how delights sidle up to us,
unannounced.

69

MISSING SPEECH-FRIENDS

When my husband died
the truest thing that anyone said to me was
"You lose your speech-friend-
the one person you can tell anything."
Now, thirty years on,
in extreme old age,
contemporaries all dead,
that is truer than ever,
A great vast cloudlike duvet-mountain
descends on you.
You can't breathe underneath.
You burst with the need to unload
the trivia, the odd cattiness, mockery.
Yes, you are permitted to voice
worries, anxieties and receive reassurance
but never, ever just to talk freely
without meeting pursed lips, disapproval, withdrawal.
You must remember always to censor all you say.
Feels like a struggling suffocation.
And I remember with guilt

my father, slowly dying,
responding always to "How are you?"
with "Still alive."
It was many years too late
before I recognised the plea
to talk about his approaching death.
And there are those-
pity those-
for whom marriage provides
no speech-friend.

70

UNEASY LANDSCAPE

It's as if
a beloved landscape turns ominous.
Moorland air, once sweet with birds and heather
and boisterous winds
is heavy with a faint, metallic,
alien smell.
A leaden rainbow, purple and grey,
arcs the sky.
The long views over farming lowlands
welcoming homewards,
have become again a field full of folk,
but angry folk, uneasy, uncertain,
mistrusting leaders,
who gallop about still,
themselves uncertain, asserting certainties,
but knowing they do not know
how to order again
this disordered world.

71

PERSONAL NARRATIVE

From a bus, looking down,
rush-hour ants stream
over London Bridge.
Above them a miasma of stories
buzz like Scottish gnats.
Each scurrying Lowry figure
carries in his head a tale
intricate, full of surprises,
like a Dickens plot.
Stories of great ones are researched,
recorded, discussed.
From them we know
the importance of detail,
the vagaries of memory
and interpretation.
Do we believe Hardy?
or Emily? or Florence?
Dwellers in remote places too,
where everyone's business is known,
their foibles are remembered,

exploits recounted,
foolishness mocked.
Some are recorded in place-names –
Eana, who, a thousand years ago,
ploughed a field at Enfield.
People's histories rarely make
a straightforward narrative.
They intertwine with those before and after
and those alongside,
more like a tangle of knitting wool
and knotted golden chains.
When you try to unravel the threads,
when you know what you need to ask
the people who could tell you
are dead.

Only a god could hold in his head
tales as multitudinous
as sands on the shore.
Perhaps that is why men had to invent him –
as a repository of their stories.

72

LISTENING TO SHOSTAKOVICH

Home from grandchildren, I listen to "Babi Yar"
and every murdered baby bears the face
of my baby grandson;
every trusting child
led by the hand to the "showers"
or, at Babi Yar, to the cliff-edge
is my granddaughter.
Sombre choirs lament
irreparable and unendurable loss,
lament the despair of survivors,
the few, the very few survivors,
hurt in body and mind,
knowing the world a bitter and evil place
where such things can be done.

I have been to Babi Yar, the place
on the outskirts of Kiev,
a taxi-ride from the quay.
I have climbed the monument,
talked to the half-crazed old Jew

who sits and begs and tells you,
over and over, "Ich war hier."
I expected a place remote and secret, hidden in a forest
but Babi Yar is just a suburban park;
across the road are shops and homes;
the woods, into which a few, a very few, escaped
are just a narrow strip of trees in parkland.
The ravine itself is undramatic now,
the level raised by all that is buried under.

I have been to Babi Yar
but that was before I became a grandmother,
before I knew that every murdered child would be my
child,
every lost baby my murdered grandchild.

73

MARCHING

Marching is for soldiers, right?
and for small boys waving flags,
neat, precise, disciplined?
Wrong.
Marching is also for citizens,
making their point.
Not really marching at all,
more a slow shuffle
with many stops,
on and off the kerb,
tripping over barriers,
chaotic, anarchic, noisy,
inspired by many motives,
under many banners:
Anti-fascist, CND, Peace not War,
for, or against, fox-hunting
down with Mosley, apartheid,
Thatcher, Trump,
past the smell of police horses,
shields protecting eyes

and formidable hooves,
past lines and coaches of police,
yellow-coated, watchful,
neat, disciplined,
somehow always vaguely,
supporting the wrong side.

74

ODE TO MAN, ISLE OF

All day the tricksy, teasing sea
silvers the bay with moonlight
then retreats, shifting black bars,
iridescent circles
that mirror clouds above.
You are as foreign, Man,
as many far-distant lands;
witness three cliff-top pastures
crowded with goats, horned goats.
Like Americans, your natives boast
the first, the biggest, the oldest
something or other.
Justified by size
Not even a dot on a world map
yet the first in the world
to give women the vote,
but more tax-haven millionaires
than somewhere or other –
a matter for boasting?
You could boast

variety of public transport –
steam trains, electric trains, mountain railways,
horse-drawn trams, buses
run alongside, crisscross,
hooting and whistling warnings,
carry us through remote and varied landscape –
Cornish cliffs and deep wooded chines,
Scottish heather and limestone,
Mediterranean palm-trees.
Far away, lost in dark cloud,
I can make out a coastline
that must be Ireland.
I can see why your children love you.
Maybe I'll come back one day
on the ferry from Liverpool to 'mainland',
the long sunset running alongside,
and travel the narrow-gauge railways,
chugging through fuschias,
and the buses, whose drivers feel no need
for locked, protective glass.

75

LIONS IN TRAFALGAR SQUARE

In Trafalgar Square
the polyglot tourists
don't feed the pigeons anymore.
They scramble on the lions,
fall off Nelson's base,
discuss the occupant
of the fourth plinth,
admire displays; today
iconic phone boxes,
bizarrely decorated.
The lions survey it all
like tolerant grandparents
dignified, benign,
oblivious of people
who sit on their heads,
are photographed
riding their backs
embracing their noses.
The square retains its grandeur.

76

NEW YORK

New York was a city of fable,
Full of names as familiar as Piccadilly
But unattached to any reality.
Now, Madison Square Garden is our landmark,
Opposite our apartment,
Bloomingdale's - that's where you bought your bag.
We know how to find our way about the Met,
Where to find the rest-rooms
Or coffee, before hearing Domingo.

Edith Wharton's girls aspired to East Side.
Arthur Miller's immigrants crossed Brooklyn Bridge.
A wrong turn -
Light the Bonfire of the Vanities.
Central Park was a name of terror,
Now it's an Autumn stroll
Between the Frick and the Natural History -
But don't linger after dark.
Manhattan is an island
We circle in a boat.

The Bronx and Harlem you still explore
Only on a guided tour
But prosperity is moving back
And the brownstones are elegant
In the October sun.
Now, they say, Brooklyn is the place of danger.
In Grand Central Station
I sat down -
And drank a coffee.

77

IGNORANCE?

Two young boys carried a milk crate
through the school playground.
They were joshing each other
in the language of computers.
I couldn't do it.
Could you?
Each generation thinks the next ignorant
because what they need to know
is different.
My father was not taught English at school –
a gentleman could of course speak his own language.
What mattered was his knowledge
of Greek and Latin.
Now even the content of a degree course
can be unrecognisable
to an earlier graduate –
my English studies knew nothing
of post-modernism, existentialism.

Perhaps it should inculcate
a healthy scepticism
about the expertise
of contemporary pundits,
medical, scientific, archaeological.

78

IMAGINATION'S LIMITS

If you have ever wondered
what it would be like
to live the life of a goldfish
or a goldfinch or a golden retriever
then reflect how little you can imagine
what it would be like to inhabit the body
of someone closest to you
but of the opposite sex:
to bleed monthly. And then stop.
or to own a member
with its own compelling needs and demands,
not entirely under its owner's command,
demands which linger long after they appear to others
to be inappropriate,
to provide milk like a cow,
to have a voice which suddenly
and out of one's control
drops two octaves,
to discover that clitoris, nipples or penis
can be aroused to excitements

not entirely imaginable to one's partner;
to learn that in many countries
and in most periods of time
your sex confers automatic status and authority
or, just as automatically,
relegates you to a subservient role,
also to a ridiculous propensity
for anything small and helpless,
a puppy, a kitten, even a baby crocodile,
to elicit maternal feelings.
And if by now you are congratulating yourself
"Yes, yes, I do understand"
then test your imagination's capacity
to inhabit the bodies of those
whose desire is aroused
by what the rest of us perceive
to be abnormal, immoral or abhorrent.
Can you still retain compassion?

79

EASTERTIME IN CRETE

Eastertime in Crete.
The old men sat on the beach,
talking and turning, turning the spit
on which the Easter lamb
cooked slowly all day.
Woodsmoke drifted along the promenade,
the smell of the herbs, the roasting meat.

We walked up into the hills.
Blue sea glittered far below,
wide blue sky above, scent of wild thyme,
crushed under our feet.
Insects buzzed and hummed.

We walked too far, needed a snack,
not much, thinking of roast lamb to come.
We had water and hard-boiled eggs,
painted dark red, handed out in the town,
from their baskets, by Girl Guides in uniform.
I said if this were a novel or film,

someone would arrive out of nowhere
and invite us to sit and drink wine
in the courtyard, in the cool of his castle.
With that, a little red car
came chug-chugging up the sandy track,
passed us, stopped.
A woman got out, rummaged in the boot,
came back down the track,
offered us, with hospitable gestures
an Easter delicacy, cool and a little sharp.
We sat among the maquis and picnicked.

In Crete, myths and legends linger, take shape.

80

HUGS

The poet spoke of her grief at the death of her mother.
Four years on, she still dreams,
recalls her in a golden light.
Listening, I felt again the deprivation
as when Paul Robeson sang,
"Sometimes I feel like a motherless child"
or when a student in a drama exercise
produced a tiny pot of embrocation.
The smell brought back for her
memories of warmth, security,
sitting on her mother's lap
while some childhood pain
was rubbed better.
Suddenly I had to fight back tears,
envying that memory.
Something went wrong in our bonding.
Later it was compounded
by her bullying and nagging of my father.
Later still I realized
how the traumas of her own life

had harmed her.
But the damage had been done already;
hers was the Truby King generation,
taught it was wrong to kiss or cuddle4
babies or small children.
The wickedness. To deprive mothers and children
of something so natural, so heart-warming.
I knew intellectually that I was loved
but I have no recollection of ever being
kissed or cuddled. If I fell over, I waited,
not for comforting arms but for the scolding voice.
Presented with her grandchildren,
she would reach out,
then hold back, saying,
"I don't believe in hugging babies"
and I was left in terror
that my deprivation
would prevent me from giving
my own children and grandchildren
the warmth and loving security
all babies need, and children.

THE EVE OF PASSOVER

The Eve of Passover
and I have a message
from a friend in Israel
about to celebrate a strange Passover
in lockdown.
But Jewish history is full of times
of danger and fear and widespread suffering.
It is the last few decades
of peace, and, for some, plenty
that are the exception.
And now a plague has come
to attack the whole world.
Let us hope its aftermath
will be some kind of unity.

82

LONDON CHANGES

So it was a lovely day.
late Autumn.
a last farewell to Summer,
warm enough to lunch out
in a courtyard,
with wasps.
We would, in the past,
have flocked to the countryside:
Epping Forest, the sea.
Today we celebrate the sun
in London:
a procession of river-boats,
packed tight, a sea of heads;
strollers thick along the South Bank,
busy tables outside each pub or café
sunglasses everywhere.
London has changed, relaxed.

ROY CAMPBELL'S HORSES

Led by your poem, Roy Campbell,
we rode the white horses of the Camargue
and a miserable, flea-bitten lot they were, Roy Campbell,
as they stumbled, heads drooping, dull-eyed,
through that land of marsh and mirage,
of bulls and flamingos, of sunshine
and the salt inroads of the sea.
Then, as the setting sun
shimmered pink on the waves,
a gypsy girl rode a stallion
through the froth of foam
at the edge of the sea.
Her long dark hair streamed behind her,
and the horse's white mane
and the horse's white tail.
She rode him bareback
and his hooves danced,
hardly touching sand or ripples,
a flying horse,

his element the air.

Then, at last, we saw with your eyes, Roy Campbell.

84

WHAT LIES WITHIN ME?

Actors and writers, it is said,
must dig deep within themselves
for traces of the characters
they want to portray.
I learned the pressure to conform to the crowd
when I surprised myself on the towpath
chanting "Oxford! Oxford!", loudly, urgently,
along with the rest.
A sinister memory goes back to childhood,
primary school.
A fat, unpopular boy was arraigned
before the whole class.
The teacher denounced his crimes
and the class joined in:
"And he did this!," "And he did that!"
We sensed he was going to be caned.
There was a nasty excitement, anticipation
in the room. We closed in
like hounds slavering for the kill.
Then we watched.

Even just afterwards I felt uneasy,
queasy about it.
Now I think of all those torturers,
Inquisitors, SS, Guantanamo Bay guards.
Does that nasty excitement
become an addiction?
Does some childhood mis-education
set them on that ugly path?
What hidden capacities
lurk within us all?

85

METAMORPHOSES

Victoria, bejewelled, bejowled,
squats unremarked
in small-town squares
and railway stations.
Costume museums display
her elephantine drawers
(Cheap in the antique trade
since she wore
a new pair every day)
and yet in Dorset,
in quiet Athelhampton,
her statue ends
a shaded walk.
Soft, gentle, young,
her shy curves lichen-veiled,
this is the She
evoked young Dickens'
half-serious passion.

Did Cranach's Eve so change?

Thrust out of Eden
to bear and age and thicken,
did she see turkey wattles
and purple veins
ruin her young translucent flesh?

There is another way.
Perhaps Eve, Eden-bereft,
changed her religion,
lit the Beltane fires,
became The Great Mother
and in crimson and gold - a diva's raiment –
learned to celebrate in dance
love, fertility and magic.

86

OLD AGE ANTICIPATED

Old Ma Grimble
Used to be nimble
"When she were young"
They say.

Old Man Ware
Sits in his chair,
Does nothing but stare,
Eyes on a scene
Far away.

"Did I ever tell
How we went through Hell
Back in the Blitz?"
He'll say.

What'll it be
Like when it's me
With nothing to do all day

But live in a Home
And sit in a chair
And stare at the old T.V.?

87

STARS

Night. In the desert.
And the sky
so spangled with stars
they seem to elbow each other,
overlap.
And each of those
uncountable spots of light
is a world? A universe?
A sight I long to see,
will never see now
though some frosty Winter nights
in Yorkshire came near.
Now I am grateful
that television transports me
to all the places I missed
in my days of travel.

88

TARTAN NOSTALGIA

Rich Americans and Canadians
with Scottish names
fill hotels in Fort William and Mull,
crowd the tourist shops of Skye and Ross,
buying their clan badges,
tartan presents for grandchildren
in Ohio, Toronto,
Balamory stories for small children
in Texas, Oklahoma.
They sign their names proudly,
proclaiming their ancestry,
search out the glens and hills of their forebears,
order kilts in their clan tartan
to wear on Burns Night back home.
Through rain-swept coach windows
they admire incomparable scenery.
Do they mourn the traces of croft and potato patch
left from the Clearances?
Do they hear the wails of women
that make every glen a Glen of Weeping?

Do they see the blood on the wool
of the black-faced sheep,
cropping every valley and hillside –
the White Plague that drove their ancestors
to starvation on the sea-shore
or cholera on the emigrant ships,
the White Sails that left Wick and Thurso
more crowded than African slave-ships,
whose cargo, after all,
had a market value, if it survived the voyage.

I hope some of the hoteliers and shopkeepers
now harvesting this romantic nostalgia
descend from the few crofters who remained
but I doubt it;
Lowland shepherds, Southern speculators
who once moved into the emptied glens –
they are the people ready to reap
this rich harvest.
Still, it's good to know
that these very Camerons,
Mac this and Mac that
with a sentimental desire to eat porridge and haggis,
hear the pipes, wear the kilt,
even toss the caber,
must mean that some of those
home-sick, fever-ridden, starving,
bewildered and betrayed clansmen ancestors
did make good.

89

CRISIS QUANDARY

My garden blooms as never before.
Hollyhocks arch above the gate.
Around the doors, lilies scent the air.
Gooseberries and blackcurrants jostle for space.
Painted Ladies dart and glint
 and chase each other across the lawn,
all delighting in this phenomenal summer
of alternating heat and rain.

My pleasure is curdled with guilt;
how can I enjoy all this rich growth
when it spells Climate Crisis as clearly
as stranded polar bears
melting sea-ice
and bits of our world
already rendered uninhabitable?

How can I enjoy my moment of pleasure
as catastrophe approaches
faster than our worst fears?

90

CLOSING DOWN

One by one the lights go out.
One by one the shops shut down,
the flowers fade.
Farewells are mostly sad.
Some come sooner than others:
never more to ride a horse,
climb a mountain,
see that glint of attraction
in a man's eyes.
Just a few are welcome –
no more childbirth.
A few give freedom –
no-one expects me to march, campaign,
deliver leaflets.
And mostly, politely
I count my blessings –
long life, children, grandchildren
interesting work, opportunities.
All true, but underneath
I rage against the closing down of life.

I want to go on
growing bright flowers,
hugging babies.
There are lands I haven't seen,
books I haven't read,
music I haven't played.
Above all I want to know
how the story continues,
what becomes of my family,
what becomes of the world.
Life is a page-turner,
then the book is snatched way
before the dénouement.

91

SURPRISE

Driving remote country lanes
I watch always for road-kill.
It tells what one might see
live in the undergrowth,
like the wild-cat
that sprang snarling
across a mountain trail
in Scotland,
so I was surprised
in a steep narrow green tunnel of a road,
far from anywhere,
to see a lively chubby little animal
rolling and twisting and turning
down the steep hill
towards the labouring car.
Finally I had to stop
to avoid running over -
a haggis.
And who was hidden,

watching and laughing
I wondered.

92

TRUE LOVE

It was only a matter of time
before we became lovers.
But that, somehow,
slowly brought to an end
our friendship.
Why? I wonder.
Perhaps she had made it
a little too easy.
Perhaps the tantalising mystery
of her clothed body
was more enticing
than the naked reality
with its appendix scar,
one nipple retracted,
a mole on the other breast.
Even our fierce political arguments
ceased to be exciting.
I began to make excuses,
missed appointments,

forgot to answer emails,
longed to escape,
found at last my true love,
I think.

93

SYLLABUS FOR AGEING

You have to be clever to be old.
They should do degrees in it.
The entrance exam is in negatives –
no addictions, cream cakes,
life-shortening diseases.
Once in, you learn in modules:
there is *Recognition*: when to use a stick,
hearing aids, give up driving;
there is *Design*: avoid plastic rain hats,
tight perms, head scarves, ankle socks with skirts,
Joan Collins make-up;
Mindfulness: make lists, check diary,
chant the name of the thing
you have gone to fetch from the kitchen,
remember that A-P-H-A-S-I-A does not spell
Alzheimer's;
Maintenance: physical – everything needs
lubricating, exercising, servicing
and mental – the world changes rapidly
and old age can be long –

learn new things;
Philosophy: everything *isn't* getting worse –
each generation thinks that –
only global warming makes it different for us;
forget your former eminence –
you are what you are;
remember that, in the whole history
and breadth of the world,
old age is a rare privilege.

94

TOBY JUG

My father had a Toby jug,
passed down through the family,
his favourite of all his antiques.
A convivial fellow, the jug, warty,
foaming tankard in hand.
Lift the black crown of his hat
and it is a drinking-cup.
Now, my father's great-grandson
is called Toby.
He began life as Jake,
then his mother decided
he was not a Jake but a Toby
so we all had to unlearn
his first name
and now his mother often calls him
Toby Jug.

95

FRIENDS

You choose your friends, they say,
but your family is wished upon you.
Not always so.
Some friends you inherit too
from long-dead partners.
Some are the detritus
of long-ago playground friendships.
Some cling like a drowning bather
out of her depth.
As you issue or accept
the unwilling invitation
you wonder if they too are thinking,
"Oh dear, I suppose I must."
What's to do?
You can't say,
"I'm sick of your endless moans
about your neighbours I've never met.
I wouldn't mind being a listening ear
for all your health worries
if just once in a visit,

just once,
you would listen to me
without interrupting."
I haven't the heart.
Or the courage?

"Hello-o-o! How nice to see you!
Do come in!"

96

AUTUMN AGAIN

I think I am tired of Autumn.
Perhaps I have seen too many -
Those repetitious Autumn leaves.
Can one tire of Autumn?
Of tawny colours reflected in lakes?
Of greenfinches, goldfinches, returning to gardens?
Well, but, what about drizzle, fog,
Slippery roads, pavements, railway tracks,
Sordid rubbish drowning in gutters?

If you tire of Autumn,
Are you tired of life?
Are there things you don't tire of?
Like freshly-ground coffee,
Compliments,
A child's kiss,
The smell of bacon cooking,
A baby held warm and close,
Home.
Not time to hand in my cards yet.

97

A CONVOCATION OF BIRDS

In Epping Forest
I followed a strange sound.
It led me to a huge tree,
brilliant with bright green flowers.
But the flowers were birds,
a myriad of green woodpeckers
jostling along every branch,
all declaiming loudly,
one against the other –
A Parlement of Foules.
Were they contending
for some avaian laureateship?

98

DU FU

Tonight on TV
I listened to the poems
of China's greatest poet,
Du Fu. They spoke to our condition today.
He lived a life much akin
to our world now,
full of change, fear, the unexpected.
Yet Du Fu lived
more than a thousand years ago.
He died in 770 AD – the age of Beowulf.
Chinese children today learn and revere
and recite his poems.
He leaves a legacy
of the importance of poetry.

99

STARGAZING

Astronomers are become poets;
with simile, metaphor, analogy
they endeavour to make us imagine
unimaginable distance, size, time, speed –
more stars in the Universe
than all the grains of sand
on every beach on Earth.
Like all poets, they seek to share
the beauty that they see –
planetary rings, colour,
the behaviour of light.
We envisage them, the astronomers,
as solitary, nocturnal stargazers
but they probably work in a team,
their chief excitement
changing figures on a computer screen.
When they let their imaginations fly free
they are brothers to fiction-writers,
conjecturing that

maybe there really are
parallel universes,
Maybe everything that could happen
does happen, somewhere.

100

SWANS OVER ORPINGTON

After three weeks,
on this wet Monday morning,
the window is still cracked
in great York-stone pieces,
spreading clumsily
from the three holes
made by airgun pellets.
At night the yobs use
the lighted windows of the college
for target-practice.
No, not Belfast –
Orpington, the suburbs.
And anyway,
it's hard to see out of the windows;
they haven't been cleaned
for several years –
a ten-storey building
and it's not safe to clean the windows.

Today, through the drizzle,

seven swans flew high
above the council estate,
purposefully, rhythmically, winging
towards the crowded lake in the park.
And before the excitement dulled,
more riches,
a great number flew past,
uncountable, like starlings or stars,
unbelievable.

And then they were past
and the glass was more dirty
and the cracks more ugly
and Monday more glum
and I thought vaguely of swans of Coole
but the students to whom I'd said,
"Look! Look!" gave the swans
only a quick glance,
too engrossed, alive, eager,
creating a play.

101

BEERSHEBA

"Where did you buy your shirt?"
"In the Beersheba camel market."
Clearly you don`t believe me
But this shirt recalls for me
A day of heat
When we ventured alone
By service bus -
No tourist trip -
To Abraham`s city.

So much as glance
At their women
Where they sat
Huddled in black,
Facing the pick-up trucks
And the Bedouin spat
A neat accurate warning
Towards our feet.

We could have bought

Camel calves,
Tethered for sale
Beneath the high-rise flats.
The carousel
Circled endlessly,
Blaring out `La Ronde`,
And I haggled
Amicably
For this shirt

MOONDANCE

Grubby little tug on the Mersey,
Inscribed on the side, "Moondance".
Some deft-footed mariner
Made mad by moonlight
Danced on the midnight deck
Of a ship lying still
On a wide ocean,
Sparkling with phosphorescence,
Light as day with a mast-high moon,
Danced till the moon danced too.
Recalling this, hobbled by age,
Naming a little boat,
Confined to Mersey,
Called it "Moondance".

BEFORE THE SMILES COME

Before the smiles come
babies stare at us
with great solemnity,
seeming to judge us,
seeming to find frivolous
our attempts to engage with them,
as we coo and baby-talk,
smile at them, bounce them,
wave fingers, rattles.

They for their part
stare unswervingly from deep blue eyes,
then, in their own time,
satisfied they have learned
the lineaments of this particular face,
they switch attention
and refuse to meet our eyes again.

They seem so wise, so alien.
Then, when the smiles begin,

the baby looks embarrassed,
turns its head coyly,
not sure about this new skill,
essays a communicative gurgle,
no longer so certain
of its own judgement,
joins the human race.

THE NIGHT SHIFT

At dusk
The night shift takes over in the garden.
A fox trots with purpose and authority
Down its accustomed path.
A blackbird whistles a final warning.
Robins chatter a little,
Settling to roost.
Domestic cats prudently retire.
A dog, late going indoors,
Barks hysterically
At whatever alien creatures
Are taking over.
As in a hospital,
The night shift is unfamiliar,
Unpredictable.
Shadowy forms approach.
Strange cries are heard.
There is a sense of danger -
And a frisson of excitement.

MULTIVERSES

I watched a programme
in which a group of scientists
tried to make multiverse theories
comprehensible to non-scientists like me.
I felt like a cyclist desperately clinging
to the back of a bus, carried along
at far beyond my own speed,
but grateful, because they did make me
understand something of what they were on about
but what struck me most
was their joyfulness and excitement
and their constant laughter
at what they themselves called
their "weird and wacky ideas",
throwing their heads back and laughing aloud.
In a world full of anxiety, depression and foreboding, it was
great to see people so full of joy
at what they saw ultimately
as another aspect of Nature, of life,
of human development.

WEARING BLACK

Why is London in mourning?
Everyone is wearing black.
You sit in the Tube
and all the people opposite
seem to be going to a funeral.
True, there is plenty to mourn for –
the death of the NHS,
the betrayal of the young,
the damage to the planet
but does it help
to add to the gloom?
I love colour.
I like to dress in colour.
Sometimes today
I feel I must look as odd
as a man walking down Oxford Street
dressed as a bee, or a baby
or a blackbird.

107

RIVALRIES

On my lawn, a jackdaw
is bullied by a wood pigeon.
Nothing too violent, just menaced in jerks
until it gives up and flies away.
Yes, nature's red in tooth and claw all right –
it's also full of hierarchies, elites,
submissions, cold war strategies,
just like us.
A big crow is more nervous than a sparrow
because its take-off time
is slower and more laborious.
Sparrows, robins, can dart off in a second,
while pigeons recognise me as harmless
up to the last approaching metre.
Aggression helps too. And confidence.
A robin will face off something much bigger
or perch on the handle of my spade.
A blackbird avoids confrontation
but can run much faster away.
But it's not really enough to observe

how bird behaviour replicates ours.
Isn't it time we moved on a bit?
Used our superior brains
to diminish hierarchy, conflict, war,
not just to increase our weaponry
of tooth and claw?

108

FASHION DOMINATRIX

On the Fourth Plinth?
A statue to the goddess Fashion, surely?
Fashion Dominatrix.
You despise Fashion?
You still eat blancmange?
Back-comb into a beehive?>
Preface futurity with
"Come the Revolution"?
Cure by blood-letting?
Or do you eat Sticky Toffee Pudding?
Exercise in brief, heart-stopping bouts?
Believe in Market Forces?
Holiday in Croatia?
And by the time you read this, of course,
they will also be The Past
and not The Present.
Fashion in all things is ephemeral,
evanescent.
Perhaps the "statue" should be

a flickering ever-changing hologram.
That would be eye-catching indeed.
At first.

109

CATCHING FIRE

As orioles catch fire
so every Spring morning
I wake in excitement to see
what new delights my garden has to offer.
Whoever planned this garden
ordained a succession,
so that daffodils and snowdrops
are followed by intertwined camellias, pink and red,,
grape hyacinths, forget-me-nots,
a magnolia tree, true hyacinths.
Along the alleyway
a thick hedgefull of yellow blossom
hides the fence.
In the conservatory
pink flowers promise nectarines
and touching the roof are three strange trees
grown from a tiny cutting,
brought from the Scilly Isles.
The leaves are glossy black fingers

surrounding a bright green centre.

And later there will be roses, fruit
and asparagus spears.

110

TRAINSPOTTERS

We stick to our kind –
a shoal of sardines, million-strong –
think like our kind –
starlings weaving swift
gigantic patterns in the sunset –
assert as certainty
opinions in the papers
we all read.
Then we spot the trainspotters –
two or three men at the far end
of a long platform
where nobody else goes –
anoraks, hoods, notebooks in hand.
They are still –
everyone else is hurried,
purposeful.
Occasionally, a wave of excitement
animates the group.
Numbers are noted.
Their interest, their esoteric knowledge

is as alien to me,
as impenetrable,
as the life of an Amazonian villager,
of a stoat, a mole.
We are not all the same.
Even the friend I know well
has a strange, a different world
inside his skull.

111

THE HANDKERCHIEF TREE

Overhanging the banks of the Nile
a handkerchief tree,
last seen at Wisley.
Paper-white the flowers hang,
extended diamonds,
spaced in patterns,
decorating the tree.
But wait!
This tree is dead
and the handkerchiefs live
and fly and flutter,
circle away and back,
a tree full of egrets,
settling to roost
for the night.
The boat glides on
and look!
another egret tree,
the same grey dead ghostly branches,
decorated with birds,

like a Christmas tree
hung with baubles.
In a world of lush green
why do they choose
only these two dead trees?

Now the wings are still,
settled for the night.
Only one hurrying latecomer
flies in,
black now,
against the Nile sunset.

112

REVERSE METAMORPHOSIS

Oh those pale mourning sweethearts of WW1,
with what reverence and compassion they are remembered,
their lives crumpled in a telegram.
But they lived on, those slight, romantic figures,
lived on in a world short of men,
lived on to become thickset, tweedy women in brogues
who shared flats and called each other by surnames,
lived on to teach my generation in the Thirties
and be the butt of nasty, unthinking jokes
in newspapers, comic postcards, schoolroom whispers.
"Sex-starved spinsters" we called them.
To comedians they were man-hungry vampires,
ugly, unlovable.
How cruel we all were,
how unjust.

113

RECOVERING FROM 'FLU

'Flu retracts its long reluctant claws,
a dying monster,
still, as it goes, drawing blood.
Don't trust its demise;
it jerks alive again
long after you think it dead.
But now at last it's truly gone;
you cannot prod it awake.
You venture into the sunshine,
gently try your muscles,
breathe deep,
return to the world.

ORIGANO

Tendrils of green origano
curve delicately across the marble
of my kitchen shelf.
Its perfume, equally delicately,
titillates my nose.
The face of the Indian woman lit up
when she caught its scent.
She became my guru,
telling me of its curative properties,
urging me to breathe it in deeply –
it would clear my mind.

All this excitement at an encounter
at a supermarket check-out.
So now the scent of the origami
and its beauty
pleasure me,
inspire also, a certain respect.

TERRIBLE COMMANDS

My mother stretched out her arms
to embrace her first grandchild
and then drew back.
"I don't believe in hugging babies."
and I remembered how
I was never hugged as a child.

When I married, I needed lots of simple hugs
as well as ones of love.
What a wicked thing to teach mothers
and it was not me alone,
most of my generation remembered a childhood without
hugs and cuddles.

Oh, the terrible commands
that have been imposed on people:
"He is ailing. Bleed him."
A girl is of marriageable age
cut her, lest she enjoy sex.
An old woman has learnt the healing power of herbs

Go drown her – she's a witch.
A boy sings beautifully,
a high tenor.

Cut off his balls so his voice doesn't break.
So what appalling things do we command today
To fill our descendants with horror?

116

HORSES OF THE CAMARGUE

We sat in a quiet suburban circle
and shared poetry.
Somebody read Roy Campbell's poem
about the white horses of the Camargue
and it all came flooding back to me
and I told them how
some sixty years ago,
inspired by that poem
I holidayed in the Camargue
and we rode the white horses
and saw the wild Camargue and the mirages
and the black line along the horizon
which was the fighting bulls.
But the horses we were given to ride
were flea-bitten, saddle-sore,
too spent to raise their heads.
Then at sunset we walked along the beach
and a gypsy girl came down,
riding a stallion bare-back.
First she let his hooves

dance in the ripples of the sea,
too proud to tread the ground,
then she galloped him along the beach,
his mane and tail, and her long hair
streaming behind
and Campbell's poem came alive.

117

WOBBLY MEMORY

When you are as old as I am
Memory leads you a wobbly dance.
Museum-pieces are objects
familiar from childhood –
mangles, dishes for butter and jam,
Liberty bodices.
Events like wars
that are History to others
are childhood memories.
The Depression is an uncle
always out of work,
your mother answering the phone
to another desperate plea for money.
The Spanish Civil War meant
collecting for milk for Spanish babies,
a school debate,
understanding that this was a different war,
where the established government,
now under attack, was of the Left,
of the people,

not, as was usual, the other way round,,
grasping that the bombs
were probably our future,
being deeply impressed
when our Classics mistress
brought back a husband,
a colonel in the Republican army,
glamorous in tricorne hat
and swirling black cloak.
And WW2 was our war –
evacuation, the sound of bombs whistling down,
initial fear of gas, fear of imminent invasion,
shrapnel banging on the shelter door,
snores drowning sleep
in a Morrison shelter.
All these are vivid as yesterday
but to follow-up questions
Memory often refuses any answers,
and so with post-war life –
singing nursery rhymes
to a baby great-grandson,
seeing him suckle
brings back vivid physical memories
of feeding your own
But in what room?
Wearing what clothes?
No, Memory does not permit
follow-up questions.

118

BORN-AGAIN

Born-again non-smokers
Stare with disdain
At groups of exiled puffers
Huddled in the rain.

Convert vegetarians
Ostentatiously proclaim
They never eat dead animals
And you should do the same.

Successful slimmers look askance
At anyone who's overweight
And leave their hostess' efforts
Hardly touched upon their plate.

Born-again non-gamblers
sanctimoniously declare
The Lottery is immoral
And betting-shops a snare.

"I don't smoke. I don't drink.
What's left for me to do?"
"'P'raps you should give up boasting
And patronising too."

119

SIGNIFICANT DATES

What are your significant dates?
The dates by which you measure time?
The birth of a child? A divorce? A loss?
My father was old when he fathered me
and I am old now
so time begins or ends for me
in 1882, the year that he was born,
twelve years after Dickens died,
Victoria still on the throne,
so my father saw the advent of motor cars,
of aviation, radio, the Boer War.
He fought in WW1, a little old for it,
donned uniform again in WW2
in the Home Guard,
mounting dangerous watch
over a munitions factory.
Now I join the dwindling ranks
who lived through and remember
the Depression of the Thirties,
the Spanish Civil War, which told us,

inaccurately as it turned out,
what to expect
in the war we knew was to come.
I was an evacuee,
grown up by the end of the war,
witness to the Blitz.
What changes and what moments of history
a single life can encompass.

WHEN THE QUIET EVENING COMES

When the quiet evening comes
and summer birds and trees are still
Oh then I think of absent friends
and number them along the years.

And when the Christmas evening comes,
children in bed, excitement stilled,
Oh then we drink a quiet toast
to absent friends,
stand silent awhile,
remembering them,
thinking of those we wish were here.

A VALUABLE EMOTION

According to The New York Times
"Disgust...is having its moment."
It's the fashionable emotion to research.
Disgust is valuable; it stops us
eating, touching, smelling
things that can harm us.

If I list the things it makes us avoid
disgust will stop you reading.
Disgust must be learned; a baby
will dabble happily in its own poo.

I found my crawling baby
chewing a wood-louse.
At what age do we learn disgust?
Can it be instinctive?

Faced with a disgusting human being,
stinking, drooling, vomiting,
drunk, masturbating in public,

can we re-learn to direct our disgust,
not at our fellow human being,
rather at whatever of illness, poverty,
madness, lack of care, past history
has brought him so low?

122

PLAYTIME

"What shall we play?" I said
"Shall we play with your train?
your Teddy bear? your Lego?
your doll's pram?"
"No," you said,
"I want you to play with my feet."
So your feet were tickled
and patted and chased
and bicycled
until I found the best game of all
and I crossed and re-crossed your legs
till your feet pointed
to the four points of the compass –
North, South, East and West
while you giggled
and tried to get it right.

We did it so often
perhaps you'll never read a map
any other way.

One day, perhaps,
you'll lie on your back
on a muddy hill track,
map held above you,
sktretch out a booted leg and say,
"That way, that way,
That's the way North."

123

BASILISK

Basilisk met me
on leaf-patterned bridge
in yellow Autumn.
Basilisk froze me.
Do your children shudder
meeting that snake-eye?
Is your womb cold within you,
Spring well-water,
like, witches say,
the Devil's congress?

Or did some terrible,
ancient,
Medusa-encounter
blast you stone-sterile?

124

POETRY

When the flat Northern voice said,
"But, Miss Pitt, poetry is not to be enjoyed.
It's to be eva-a-aluated"
then all the great tumescent gods of poetry
drooped, half-masted.

But it is not so.

Poetry is a river, an ocean,
a torrent in flood.
Poetry is to be gobbled, wallowed in,
its delights being dolphin-like.
It is for reading in punts, at bus stops.
It is for shouting in baths
or against the sounding seas.
Poetry is a fur for our mind's lining,
a dark rich sable, concealing secrets,
which hop and slide sidelong into our lives,
like forgotten savours
of honeysuckle and green almonds.

Thus each experience is enriched by words
spoken in another time and stored in another place.
The heaves and surges of the brown river swell
and rise, sudden and vast beneath,
always unexpected, always closer to overwhelming
than one expects
like the mountainous breakers when one rides,
just rides, the surf.
Most like the tremendous endless nightmare,
joyous torrent, of childbirth.

Poetry too, as suddenly, casts us
on a soft quiet sandspit
lulled by the river, intensely still,
in a summer afternoon before thunder,
whence begins again the interior stir and prick of
excitement
which betokens a poem coming.

125

THE UNEXPECTED

Beauty surprises us
in unexpected places:
light playing on ripples
in the clear water
as I run my bath;
Autumn colours on peony petals
fading in borders
outside my French windows.
Sounds too:
someone who spoke no English
asked to choose the word
that sounded to him
the most melodious,
alighted on "cellar door".
One could make a sermon out of that –
about the need to look for
the unexpected redeeming trait
in those we dislike, discount, abhor.

126

EARTH

Not so long ago
you were a tin ball from Woolworth's,
garishly painted,
easily dented,
much of you pink.

Before that
you were the centre of the universe
or flat.
Men ventured towards your edges,
fearing to fall off.

Now we know you as a silvery beauty,
much of you blue,
floating in vastness,
viewed from afar
by man and camera,
shown on our screens,
easily damaged.

Unwitting toddlers,
we poisoned you,
upset your balance,
gobbled your sustenance.
Now, careless teenagers,
we know, and disregard, the danger.
The future, we think,
is a long time away,
when beautiful Gaia will die.

127

UNIVERSAL ETHICS

Geology is difficult
And algebra is hard.
English is a doddle
'cept for studying the Bard.
Arithmetic was simple
Until they called a yard
A meter and the metre
By that was somewhat marred'
But there's just one subject
That everyone can do
It's as easy as ABC.
It has a set of basic rules
On which we all agree.
So Universal Ethics I shall celebrate in song:
"I may not be artistic but I do know right from wrong."

Of course you do.
We all do
The whole world through.
I just want to put to you

A question or two:
Is it wrong to cross a picket line?
Is it right to eat beef stew?
Is smoking a right or a wrong?
Is it all right
To keep tigers in a zoo?
Faced with the choice
As in WW2
Do you sacrifice your country – or your child?

And what about the things that other people do?
The Saudis cut thieves' hands off.
They think we should do so too.

Isn't in nice
We all know in a trice
Just what's the right thing to do?

128

THE DEATH OF GAIA?

It's December, yet,
thanks to climate change,
my silver birch is in full
golden glory. There are
roses in bloom, marigolds,
a primrose.
The builders next door
are working in warm sunshine..
I feel such guilty pleasure
at enjoying signs
that mean already
devastation in some parts of the world
and, if we don't act to stop it now,
the eventual death of Gaia,
our beautiful planet.

129

MERRY WIDOWS?

Merry widows? No.
Jolly sometimes,
joining things,
supporting each other,
going, white-haired, on coaches,
for seaside jaunts,
acknowledging compensations –
no more snoring,
free choice of television programmes.
Don't pursue that thought too far though;
it crumples to dust in the mind
like faded rose-petals.

130

AQUARIUM

Saskia, on her first birthday,
at the London Aquarium,
presses starfish fingers against the glass,
jigs up and down with excitement,
reaches out to grasp handfuls
of tiny swimming jewels,
exchanges intimate communion
with a lobster, an octopus,
a conger eel, a shark.
None of this she will remember,
being too little,
but perhaps,
when she is old enough for stories,
hearing tales of mermaids, silkies,
and the coral palaces
of sea-kings' daughters,
she may feel a dim sense
of coming home.

BLUES

What the Blues sing
Is the human condition,
The woes of the world
Repeated through history,
With no simple harmonic resolution,
So when people lament, justly,
The wrongs of the Palestinians
And demand, unjustly,
That the Jews and Tel Aviv
Be cast into the sea,

I think of Broadway,
The Indian trail,
Snaking through New York`s neat grid
And imagine the skyscapers toppled
And the land given back
To buffalo and tepee
But it isn`t going to happen.
For all the shameful history

Of dispossession, betrayal, duplicity,
You can ameliorate -
You can`t reverse.
Modern music doesn`t go back to the same key
But to something - unexpected.

132

PRAISE

"Praise the Lord" said the preacher.
Praise people, say I.
I like being praised;
I reckon others like it too
so I give praise.
It's an easy gift.
It costs you nothing
but a moment's thought, a look,
because it must be genuine
or it's worthless,
except, maybe,
for the demands of courtesy
and kindness –
"Do you like my new hat
for my daughter's wedding?"
Yes, of course I do. Whatever.
But where you can
notice and praise
the new dress,
the baby's content,

the prize won,
the speech made
you give and receive
a warm glow.
Praise is a garland, a halo,
a protective coat,
an embrace.
I praise praise.

133

BUT…

I've never been one to tell tales,
But you know our new neighbours, the Gales?
Well, he's often away
And she's busy all day
Entertaining successions of males.

I've never been one to tell lies
But I burned all my cake-show mince pies,
So just as a try-on
I bought some from Jo Lyon
And they won me the judges' first prize.

I've never been one to complain
But, Doctor, I've got such a pain.
It goes right through my middle
And whenever I piddle
I have to go straight back again.

I've never been one to take more
Than the time I'm allowed on the floor.

But if you've a moment
No, don't go away!
I'll read you a poem I wrote yesterday,
And one more,
And another
And then three or four,
Till the audience grows restive
And makes for the door,
And the desperate chairman cries,
"Madam, no more!"

Then I stop.

134

GOLDEN BALL

On the shores of the Yangtze
men stood, motionless as herons
arms embracing a huge
imaginary globe –
a form of T'ai Chi.
My T'ai Chi ball is smaller –
the size of a human head.
It is made of gold,
perforated in strange designs,
the metal warm to my touch.
Each time my hands form its shape
it glows light
and my heart lifts.

DRAWING CURTAINS

Pottery in a dark room.
Its colours lost.
No delicate flowers.
Draw back the curtains.
Light floods in.
All is restored..
Not so easy
to draw the curtains
that darken the mind.
Light creeps in gradually,
over time,
needing help.
The world looks well again
but uncertainly,
not to be entirely trusted.

ALTERNATIVE

In the Hockney exhibition
were several pictures
lovingly depicted
of men's naked bums,
the owners prone, expectant.
And why not?

Straight woman that I am
it is hard to imagine the erotic appeal
but I was glad to see them there.
Painters and sculptors for millennia
have portrayed the breasts of women
for the delectation of straight men.

This alternative allure
enlarges our imagination.
And now we are invited
to enter the mind
of the still figure, pool-side,

regarding the underwater swimmer
in the water below.

FASHIONS CHANGE

My babies were parked in prams,
left to the entertainment of moving leaves.
Fresh air was everything.
Today's grandbabies sit on my lap,
survey the activity of the kitchen,
swivel dark blue eyes
to stare at my face,
taking in a being who is Not Mother.
They cry. They fall asleep.
They dream, twitching like puppies.
(What does a three-week-old dream of?)
Tired backs rest in Moses baskets
but not for long.
Soon they demand attention again
and a view of the world.
It's a lot more stimulating
than moving leaves.
Are we raising a generation of geniuses?

THE SILK SHOP – TIMOR MORTIS

This shop sells a wealth of materials –
gingham, velvet, sarsenet, denim, damask, muslin,
poplin, linen, corduroy, silk,
but the customer is not allowed to say,
"I want two yards, please"
or "five metres"
"I need enough for a kilt"
or "A sari."
The silk flows through my fingers,
heavy with its own richness.
Like a cat,
it falls always
into new curves of grace.
Lights touch it.
Colours shift –
deep greens of forest,
fire, sky, jewels,
the glint of stars.
It whispers, susurrates.
It is measured out for me

on the brass rule
built into the counter,
yet I am not to know
when the measuring hand will stop.
Shall I be given enough
for a doll's dress?
or a cloak?
or curtains for a great house?
before the shears
tear across the pattern,
leaving a raw edge?

139

FRUIT

Why are fruits, so delicious, so luscious,
ominous, dangerous in myth?
Eve's apple settled the fate of mankind.
A witch's apple poisoned Snow White.
A golden apple, thrown,
judged between three goddesses.
Perhaps an ancient memory lingers
of a time when our ancestors,
wandering through forests, must guess
which fruits would feed
and which kill.
Or perhaps only apples are suspect
and we can gorge safely
on peaches, pears, pomegranates –
Ah, no! Wasn't it pomegranate seeds
that did for Persephone?

140

SEEING

I stood on the Embankment
and watched a colossal dinosaur
come nodding towards me.
A second later my brain recognised its mistake
and showed me a huge truck
supporting a tall nodding crane.
It was a reminder that "seeing"
is a two-fold process –
first the eye and then the brain.
It makes you wonder
about the validity of evidence.
Do you see what I see?
Do we see the same colours?
I knew someone, blind from birth,
who "saw" colours in terms of music;
scarlet was the sound of trumpets
which seemed about right to me.
I knew all this from three years old
when I was told I must come indoors
because there was "lightning"

and I saw, quite distinctly -
I can still see them now –
a line of rose-pink, fringed lampshades
just like the one in my mother's bedroom
but stretched across the stormy sky.

141

BONFIRE

The bonfire flamed fierce and high.
Wood exploded in rifle shots.
Ash floated down in tiny flakes,
softly, silently, uniformly.
Not wanting ash on my coat
I stepped back from the circle of light.
No ash on my sleeves.
Snow, not ash!
It was snowing!
Tiny flakes fell softly, slowly,
met the fierce flames
and vanished.

142

ORCHIDS

A friend gave me orchids,
not the stiff, single kind
that used to go
with a mink coat,
a silver fox fur,
(eyes and all)
and a tiny black hat
with a veil –
Marlene Dietrich-fashion.
These are a strong colour –
magenta and white,
many-blossomed.
Buds, which will mostly not open,
the shape of ballet shoes,
instep arched,
intertwine,
creating a structure.
Sun catches curves on a glass vase,
fanning out hair-thin rays
which constantly move

like natural fibre optics.
The water becomes a mirror
for the brick-red coleus
by the window,
in turn reflected,
right way up,
in the glass of the table-top –
endless repetition
like the mirror in the painting
of Arnolfini
and his pregnant bride.

A World in A Whirlwind

The first book in this poetry collection

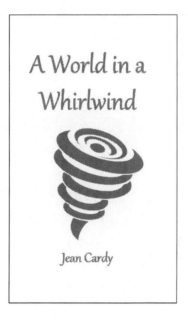

Available in eBook and Print

ABOUT THE AUTHOR

Jean Cardy was born in January 1925 and has lived a long and colourful life. She was a child at the beginning of the Second World War and emerged as an adult when it ended. Jean lives in North London and recently survived Covid-19 at the age of 96!

Jean can be contacted at:
jeancardy125@btinternet.com

Printed in Great Britain
by Amazon